IT'S ALL IN THE WORDS

AND THE NEGATIVE AFFECT THEY HAVE ON YOUR SALES

Neil Carlson

authorHOUSE®

AuthorHouse™
1663 Liberty Drive
Bloomington, IN 47403
www.authorhouse.com
Phone: 833-262-8899

Published by AuthorHouse 11/13/2020

ISBN: 978-1-6655-0655-7 (sc)
ISBN: 978-1-6655-0654-0 (e)

Think About It   You Know You Want It   May I
                         Talk It Over

IT'S ALL IN THE WORDS

I Need To Sleep On It   I Need To Talk To My Spouse

What Do You Think   **&**   Lets Do The Deal

And The Negative Affect They Have On Your Sales

I'll Let You Know   I'm Not Sure

                         I'm Just Looking

Give Me A Few Days   I Don't Buy The First Time Out

I'm Saving You Money   I Need To Shop Around

"YOU NEED TO CHANGE YOUR THINKING – IN ORDER TO CHANGE THEIRS"

Author
Neil Carlson
www.itsallinthewords.com

IF YOU NEW WHAT PEOPLE WERE THINKING -WOULD YOU HAVE MORE SALES?

_____YES _____NO

IF YOU COULD CONTROL THEIR THOUGHTS- WOULD YOU MAKE MORE MONEY

_____YES _____NO

HAVE I GOT YOUR ATTENTION? That's great!

What we need to do is get together, so I can share this information with you – so you can make a logical decision whether or not you even need this info, Is that a fair request?

_____YES _____NO

I know what you're thinking. Your thinking if what I said was fair.

I controlled your thought process – causing you to say yes.

When they say yes, you can say; Great, HOW SOON? Or you can say; Great, HOW SOON, TODAY OR TOMORROW? Never ask when.

There's more inside the book.

Call me: 623-340-2214

Thank you for taking the time to read this book. I want to thank everyone for their participation in contributing to the research and information they have provided me in the completion of this book.

My sales experience leads me to find a better way. Why sales people were losing sales. What was the reason behind, how customers responded to sales people based on what they say and the conversation they have with the customers?

The most interesting part of my journey was listening to sales people. I've found it absolutely amazing the similarities there are in the sales process from sales person to sales person and how they communicate and the words they use to try and get the sale without realizing they give people reasons not to buy.

Another aspect of my research was discovering how sales people were giving customers reasons to say NO! That alone gave me tremendous information. From that I needed to find out how to change it. I found a way just listening to what sales people were saying in response to what customers where saying.

Another aspect of my research was finding how severe sales people are conditioned. That was an incredible wake up call for me. As you'll read in the book, we're all conditioned know matter what we do. Even myself, I realized once I recognized it, it was hindering my sales. Don't get me wrong, I considered myself an excellent sales person until

I started recording myself to see if I was conditioned. That started me on my journey to discover as much about sales and selling as I could. Hence; It's, All About The Words!

I hope you find your journey as successful as I did mine.

CONTENTS

SALES, A GREAT OCCUPATION

Sales is a process of learning skills. Learning as many different types of skills as you can to become educated in and self-determined as you can be to achieve as much success as possible.

We're all born with different personality traits, which we develop over time and through contact with other people. Then are personality is enhanced as we gain knowledge and continue to improve.

At some point in time as we get older and more educated in the buying and selling process, we start to develop different selling skills, both good and bad until we come to the conclusion we need to become better. So, we try to develop better skills by reading more books and listening to tapes and CD's on selling techniques. We attend seminars and ask people in different groups about what they say and do, to get information to improve on our selling skills.

Along the way, the skills we develop determine our level of sales success. As we progress in sales and learn what works and doesn't work, we continue on with our search to become as good as we can be. Sometimes we get on the internet to find whatever we can that might help us on that journey.

Remember: It's easier for people to buy when they're selling themselves.

We look and listen for things that might sound good and appear to be better than what we do that would help us improve.

After our research, we made decisions on whether or not the information was good enough or not or we pass it by and look for more. Sometimes we take what we have learned and try to fit it into our personalities in hope that it will work the same way for us as it did from where we received it. Not always a good fit.

Sometimes we just get to the point that it just won't fit, and we move on. Then we start asking questions, why does it work for them and not for us? It certainly seems like it works for everyone else, therefore it should work for us, but alas it does not. So, after a few hours of frustration we give up and move on. On to the next research. But, we keep wondering why is it that way?

Well, probably because it's too hard to insert into our own personality or maybe our delivery is not the same as theirs is. Who knows?

There's got to be a better way to learn and find the solution we need to improve. I always wondered why people spend so much time looking at what others do and try to copy that instead of looking into themselves and figure out what's going on there. Find it within you.

What you don't realize is you have all the answers to all the problems. You just haven't taken the time to find them. I mean you truly do. Think for a minute about what you say and how you say it (this will be covered more in the book as you go along) and how you say. Then ask yourself, am I getting the answers I want to get from my customer or prospect? If, you're not, then ask or say something different that will get you what you want.

Learning to become better at what you do is finding out what it is that isn't giving you what you want.

In all my years in sales I have always try to find better ways to get people to respond the way I wanted them to respond. That took all kind of practice doing it over and over again. Recording my presentations. Listening to people and how they responded to my questions and the way the responded.

I find that you can't just read a book or listen to a tape and become the best in the world at what you do. You have to become so much more. Even this book. It will give you tons of information, but if you don't understand the reasons behind it, you won't become any better than you are now. I mean that.

So, what you should be doing is looking for all your strengths and weaknesses and determine why they are strengths and weaknesses. Then work from there. If you do, your life will change.

IT'S ALL IN THE WORDS

If you only knew how true a statement that is. Over the years I have listen to and recorded hundreds if not thousands of sales people trying to sell their products and services. I've listened to what they say and how they say it. I've listened to their exuberance and excitement only to find out they lose the sale hearing customers say, no thank you, I can't afford it, I want to think about it, let me sleep on it, I'll talk it over with my spouse, partner, give me a day or two and so on. I know you've all had that experience a time or two, so I have a question for you.

What happen?

I've always wondered about that. What happened? Especially when everything was going well and I just knew I had the sale; I knew I was going to close it. When I came to the end of the presentation I got the objection(s) Really didn't expect them either.

I asked the right questions, kept their interest in the product, did a great presentation, eve overcame some objections, but they still gave me an excuse as to why they were not going to buy. I really believed I did a very good job.

Obviously, something was missing that caused them to come up with a no or some other off the wall excuse.

I know there's a lot of training in the sales industry that covers virtually every aspect of the sales process. You know like facts, features and benefits. Over- coming objections, asking questions, how to move the sale forward and so on.

What I have never seen or heard about (not that it's not there) is the emphasis on sales language. Oh, I've gone on the internet looked at it and played some video on u-tube and heard about sales language but that's not the kind of language I'm speaking of.

The language I'm speaking of are the words we use that cause the customer to change their mind, put you off, stop listening, come up with excuses that just shouldn't be there and all of this is because of the words we use prior to the words we get back. You know the ones we don't want to hear.

What it is that YOU say that cause a negative response, what you thought you would not get. What about language skills and conditioning? You really don't hear a lot about that these days.

One always affects the other. I find that most salespeople have no idea of the impact their conditioning and verbiage has on the outcome of the sale. People sales people are so conditioned with what they say and how they say it that they can't recognize it as a problem, especially a problem that can lose the sale for them and yet it does.

What's really interesting is the sales person can't even recognize they have the problem. They'll even deny it. I think part of that reasoning is their conditioning.

We are terribly conditioned. Like putting your pants on the same way every day for years without even doing it another way. Stirring your coffee with your right hand. You do it at a comfortable rate of speed knowing you won't even spill it.

Try stirring your coffee with the other hand and do it at the same rate of speed, you find it doesn't work out as well. You'll probably make a mess at it. Why does that happen? I believe it's because we just don't think about it any longer. And that's what happens in the sales process. We just don't think about what we're so conditioned to say and do because we've done it for so long.

We don't hear it when we're giving someone a reason to say no, put us off or change their mind because we don't recognize it as a bad thing or negative thing.

It's very hard to hear what you don't recognize as negative. It's just like saying May I, as we have discussed. WE, know we're going to get a NO, but we don't recognize it until we get it.

The one thing I'm positive of is salespeople and consumers are training each other in all these problem areas.

Remember: Customers can be closed by you or closed by them. What do you think they prefer?

We're giving the consumer reasons to be negative and yet when we're not selling and where shopping we do the same thing to sales people that they do to us. We don't think about it, it's just part of our conditioning. I'm hoping this book will help you to recognize this and learn from it as a problem and to be aware.

One thing very important to remember; YOU CAN'T BREAK THEIR CONDITIONING – UNTIL YOU BREAK YOURS. The hard part of this is breaking yours until you know you have it. I would strongly recommend you work on it.

Be careful how you start the process. Once you start, be careful. Listen to how you start and what you say. It WILL make all the difference in your presentation. Don't ask for permission to do your job, it gives them the right to say NO! You'll read more about all of this as you go through the book.

There is one thing I want you to remember, this will help you change your thinking about selling. I know most all of you have heard this expression before.

"You can lead a horse to water, but you can't force him to drink"

Most of you will agree with that and you're wrong. You can force them to drink. (Change your thinking) What you need to do is make them thirsty along the way, They'll drink.

Change your thinking and you'll change there's.

ARE YOU EARNING TOO MUCH?

I love that! One of the things I've always done in my training and at seminars or works shops is ask people for a show of hands. How many people here are earning too much money?

Every time I ask a group of salespeople that question and to raise their hands, no one does. Do you believe that, no one ever does? That's quite interesting to me. That tells me many things. 1. No need any help. 2. No one asks for help. 3. No one wants any help unless they go to some one's seminar and then they pick what they think will work and move on. And yet here's the worst part of that. They forget it all in three or four days. What was the sense going in the first place? 4. I already know everything I need to know. 5. What is there left to learn? I believe I've reached the cap. REALLY??

Now, as brilliant as I am, all of that tells me if no one is earning too much money then why aren't they earning more? What's holding them back?

I've asked many people that and had one person say to me; I'm just not sure what to do. I'm not sure how to make it better. I've tried many different ways, read many books trying to find out why, asked people, and never found the right answer.

It appeared to me, it was a very easy question to ask, but a very hard question to answer and that was the most interesting thing of all. I summarized there was nowhere to go for the information. As it was, no one, had a good answer as to why?

Maybe salespeople are just not hungry enough to find out why. Maybe sales people don't really want to make more money, they're complacent. Or maybe they're just too lazy to want to work on it, that could be the answer right there.

Either way. It looks like a lot of people have just given up. Everyone wants more and very few have the initiative to get more.

To except mediocrity with visions of grandeur doesn't work for me. Maybe we're too proud to show weakness and that's why we stopped. Or, it could be because we have ego's that it prevents us from pursuing the ask to find out. That could be a good reason why. Maybe we just believe it's not possible to improve because we've tried so many other things. I've spoken to hundreds if not thousands of salespeople about this and now I'm speaking to you.

I also remember speaking with two specific people about this. One in the cemetery and funeral industry and the other one in the insurance industry. I'm using these two professions because I got the same answer from both.

I asked them what they need to learn about their profession to be great and earn too much money? They said they were great there just wasn't enough time in the day to earn more money. Wow!! I said. That's wonderful. So, for every waking hour you're selling, even during lunch and drive time? You're just going from one to the other, all day long. I asked. How many sales a day, do you get in the cemetery business? The response was, 3 to 4 a day. That's impressive. And, in that business it is. I know because I was in it. I had a day I got 11 sales. It was a very long day.

The other person in the insurance business told me she got 6 sales in a day. Her closing ratio was 99%. She virtually, closed everyone. I said you must be the best in the company (country). I couldn't believe it, she said no, there's a guy that closes more than me. I thought to myself, one of us is missing something. I decided not to pursue it any further. But what does that tell you?

I asked both this question. If you know everything about your product, how much do you know about people? What makes people tick and respond certain ways to sales people? Why do they have objections they did not have before they were being sold? Why do they put sales people off? You know, want to think about it, sleep on it, talk to spouse, need a couple of days and so one. Why do people say those things? What causes them to be brought up?

Remember: Sometimes they don't say no, they're just thinking it.

I got all kinds of answers to those questions. Surprisingly, they had some the same and many of them different. They told me they don't get those. That's when I said great! And moved on.

I figured if they knew why people said what they said and did what they did, they'd probably make a lot more money. You might want to give that some thought as well.

The reason for this book is to show you different ways to accomplish more successes. To get you to think about you and what you say and do. Try and show you that people will always give you what you ask for. If it's a no, you'll get it. I mean if you think you're asking for a yes and you get a no, you got what you asked for, otherwise you would have gotten the YES! Think about it.

I've had an awful lot of salespeople and managers say to me; Why fix it – if it isn't broken? And, I would fire right back. **"How do you know it isn't broken?"**

I would say, just because history tell you it is the way it is, doesn't mean it has to stay that way. It means you have to think of another way. Historically in the insurance industry they say; 100 phone calls to get ten appointments to make one sale, maybe two. That tells me it's definitely broken.

I did insurance for years and never made 100 phone calls to get ten appointments. I would hang myself to do that.

What I did do was find something I knew they would want to have and got them to set an appointment to get it.

The problem with a lot of salespeople and companies is they're not looking for it and that's why it's so hard. You have tons of information available, look through it all and find it and then you'll destroy the numbers. I did.

One of the most important things a salesperson can do for themselves is to change their thinking. You'll learn more about that as you go on.

THE EMOTIONS OF A SALE

And why aren't we so emotional? I found out in the earlier part of my sales career that sales and the process of sales has a lot of emotional aspects to it.

That was a blessing in disguise. At first, I didn't really realize the importance of that until it hit me one day when a customer raised her voice at me, she said that I was not listening to her (this was a wakeup call). When that happened, I took a step back and replayed the scenario in my head. She was right and then I understood why her voice fluctuation had changed so drastically.

From that point on I knew it was important to see and hear the voice fluctuation to grasp the emotions of the conversation. I also knew that her body language and her language were all tied in together. With all that information, what was I going to do with it? How was it going to help me become better?

Well, because I was so new to that discovery, how was it going to work? Well, I had to figure it out. I experimented with customers and what I did was to change my voice fluctuation and waited for the reaction. Emotions are a very natural part of our make-up. It's a natural instinct. It's an instinctive state of mind deriving from one's circumstances, mood or relationship with someone. That was the key. A natural instinctive state of mind.

Now that told me a lot of what I needed to do and what I needed to know about people, and more importantly, about how the emotions will play in sales.

We create emotions based on the language we use in selling. We create excitement, anger, sadness, disappointment, frustration and surprise. Looking at all of that, I asked myself how many of those we control or can change? Obviously, it was all of them. And how many of them have a direct impact on the selling process? Bingo! All of them again. This was a huge wakeup call for me and I was going to use them all, as many as I could in every sale. I just had to figure out how.

To me, what kind of trigger do we pull? What emotions are we creating that hurts the sale and helps the sale?

Are we using their emotions to benefit us or to hurt us? What kind of emotions and to what degree? These were questions I need to answer. Are we aware of the emotions we are creating to help the customer and ourselves?

I'll try and give you an example of the importance emotions can play in the sale.

When I was in cemetery and funeral sales I had to rely on emotions, not only to get my point across, but would also to get their thought process moving toward my direction (will get more into that as well), so I could control the process.

Here's what I use to do. I developed different degrees of emotion so I could go back and forth during the sale. I did mostly in-home sales. I would enter the home and tell the customer I am taking off my shoes as to not drag dirt in the home and leave them at the door. Then I would sit down in the living room (that was a no-no in that industry, but I proved it wrong). I would look around the room and on the walls, at pictures of the family, anything I could talk about. Then I would get to it.

You know Mr. Smith, I talk to a lot of people and the one thing I always ask, is who is going to get stuck? They would always say, what do you mean? Then I would say, well, what I mean is, when you pass someone in your family will get stuck with an untimely death and they'll have to make arrangements. Who do you want to stick with that? They're going to have to figure everything out on their own. What you want, don't want and how everything will be done and of course, who will pay? Then I would point to the pictures on the wall and say; Who's it going to be? I would pause and say; Is that what you want to do? More often than not, he would say, NO! I'm not going to stick anyone with that. Emotions are in full swing.

Then I would say, I know you don't want to do that. So, what should we do? Then I would say, Mr. Smith. I'll tell you what most people do and give them options of what start with first. Then I would say; what is it you want people to remember you by/with? People need to remember the good things, right?

It's like those shoes over there. If I leave them here, you'll remember me forever. When I put them on and leave, you'll forget about me in a couple of days. They'll be nothing there to remember this evening together.

Neil Carlson

I created different levels of emotions in people to get my point across as you need to do.

And it wasn't just to get my point across but was also to get them thinking about the importance of what we were talking about, and in the direction, I need the sale to move in. That's what was important.

What I discovered was just how important emotions played in the sales process and how important that was in getting the customer involved in the process as well.

I also realized that emotions covered a huge part of the sales process, like objections, presentations, questioning, and body language and tone of voice and eye contact.

There were so many areas of the sales process that emotions played an intricate role in it was just over whelming. It seemed as though emotions were everywhere.

How you deal with emotions can make a huge impact on the selling skills. Emotions are part of your everyday life. You deal with emotions in your job, relationships, family and friends and even with strangers you don't know. We become so conditioned to emotions, we just don't think about the role it plays.

Think about your emotions in the course of your day, you just might be surprised how involved it can become.

Try to become conscious of the level of emotion in your day to day. It could be a wonderful wake up call, for you.

I used to record my sales to hear what I was saying and the kind of response I was getting. Did it benefit me or not? Did I get the response I was listening for; from the statement I said or the question I asked? Did it serve a purpose to move the sale forward, to drive it in another direction? Was it what I expected to hear or not?

Was I giving customers reasons to say NO? Recording gave me tremendous insight into my own sales abilities. I was very thankful for that. You might want to try it in your sales. The discovery might kill you.

Emotions are for learning how to become a better sales person and a better person. How to recognize where your conversation is headed and with what degree of comfort?

Remember: We become what we think and so do they.

IF VS I

I find it really interesting listening to sales people with what they say and how they say it. Especially when they're giving customers reasons to say NO and they're not even aware of what they're doing to cause the problem.

I have found over the years most salespeople don't even hear what they're saying that cause such a problem. They don't hear what the effects are what they say has on the sales process and on the customer.

More importantly, they don't hear the effect of the words they're using and how the customer interprets the words. Even when the sales person means one thing and the customer responds to something different than what was said or thought what was said. Such confusion.

Most often than not; this happens on the phone as well. It affects the direction of the call. Meaning, is the call going where the customer wants it to go or the sales person?

Let me explain. First, I love shopping sales people. It's just amazing how conditioned they are and not even aware they are. If only they knew how that conditioning affects the outcome of the sale, especially when they thought they had it just to find out they lost it. Terrible, terrible.

I believe sales is nothing more than an action and re-action in language. And, more importantly, you always get what you ask for. Good bad or indifferent, you get it. You're conditioning greatly effects the outcome of that sale because the conditioning plays a vital role in the language you use in the process.

Here is what I hear all the time from salespeople. Maybe, you even do this. We'll see what happens. Constantly asking your customers to say no, put you off, stand you up, change their mind and so on. Once you read these you'll probably say, Oh, yeah, I say those words and you probably do the same

Tell me if this is what you say?

If I can show you a better way?
If I can save you some money?
If I can get you a deal?
If I can make life a little easier for you?
If you would try this?
If you would give it some thought?
If you do this, I'll do that?
If I can make it affordable?
You might even be able to think of more.
So, what does all this mean? What do you think?
Or better yet, what do they mean and what do they imply?

Remember: You think you're listening you just don't hear what they say.

You probably got it right but let me help you out. **IF** is a dirty word when you use it selling. It can be a good word when the customer uses it or you direct it toward the customer. Here's what I mean. **IF creates doubt! It creates doubt in your ability to do something or follow through with something.** When you say if I can, you're also saying you may not be able too. If I can show you a better way? You're saying I may not be able to show you a better way. Here's the problem as I hear it.

Can you show them a better way? Can you make it affordable? Can you save them money and so on?

IF YOU CAN, then why don't you say it? I CAN SHOW YOU A BETTER WAY!

I will. There is no doubt, as to what you can and will do, Is there?

Now **if** you have to use **if**. Use it this way. Create some doubt in the customer to prove they mean it and want it and they're serious about it. This will also give you a chance to get another "YES" from them and an easier time in closing the sale.

Remember, you need every advantage you can get to close sales and keep control of the sales process.

NOW, TRY THESE

You say; I will do this – if, you'll do that? Now it's on them, not you.

I will save you money IF you want to save money.

I will show you a better way, IF a better way is what you want?

I will make life better for you, IF you want a better life?

I'm sure you have a better understanding now and you get it, so try and change it. Sales is hard enough, don't add to the difficulty. Make it easier for yourself. Take advantage of every situation you can.

"It's all in the words," and how you use them. Be a matter of fact person. You can do it, so let them know you can.

You're creating a positive response when you say I, instead of IF. Don't create doubt in your abilities to do something.

People want to know you can and will do something, instead of a maybe or you can't.

You would want to hear the same thing too when you're buying a product or service, don't you? Be better than the rest and you'll reap more of the benefits.

MAY, I

I've always wondered why people didn't get it. In all my years researching sales people from the east coast to the west coast, they just didn't get it. I am totally confused by that. And why consumers always want to say no! Actually, I do know why.

What I found fascinating is why salespeople never hear it, or at least don't hear why they're getting all the no's. Because in my mind, if they heard the no's, as much as I did, they would want to change it immediately.

The truth of the matter is sales people don't hear what they say. Oh, I know they heard something when they spoke but they didn't recognize it. Now that I believe.

On and on it continues. It's like a driving force that keeps sales people from having a better experience with their customers. They keep right on saying it. MAY, I?

Being so conditioned to say may I gets imbedded in your brain and becomes part of your sales language and train of thought. It keeps getting reinforced as they keep saying it over and over.

Conditioning is a good and bad thing, it just depends on how you use it. If you can recognize your conditioning and why you have it and how it's used, you'll be able to make changes as you go along. We become so conditioned because of repeated use, we get to the point of not recognizing how we're affected by it and that makes it difficult to change. I'll give you an example of just how bad it can be and why it's not recognized.

We all go to the mall shopping at one time or another, unfortunately, this is where it starts. Let me give you an example of this. You're at home and you decide you need a pair of shoes, or maybe some make-up. Either way we go through a process of how the journey will start and end.

As we get ready to make our journey to the mall, we're not thinking about the shoes or the make-up, we're just going there. Then we park the car, walk to the mall, enter and walk to the store. We enter and walk to the make-up counter.

We pick up a product and our peripheral vision picks up some movement. It's coming towards us, closer and closer. (yes, that's right) it's a sales person and now it begins.

We know the conversation before it starts and we sub-consciously know the ending. The sales person says what? Yes, you're right! MAY, I HELP YOU? And, of course you respond with no thank you, I'm just looking.

Here's what I don't understand. You thought about what you wanted, took the time to drive there and park and walk into the store to find what you wanted and found it. Then a sales person enters the picture and all of a sudden you don't want it any longer because you said no thank you, I'm just looking. Why did that happen? Why did you say NO?

We do this way too many times. Everyone does it. Our conditioning and lack of trust for sales people drives us to that point. We don't want to be bother by sales people. We don't trust them, we don't like them, they just want our money, try to sell us everything. They don't care about us and so on. It is a never-ending process. On and on it goes.

So how do we change it? One of the best ways I've found to change this conditioning and the language we us in sales to record the process or to practice the presentation and play it back to hear what you're actually saying. Listening to what you're actually saying will be a wakeup call for a lot of you.

Some of you won't even believe what you're actually saying. You'll swear it wasn't you that said it. It really will be a very good learning experience. If you can't do that, then write down all the words that dictate you asking for permission> You know, may I, can I, will you, should, could would, how about and what if?

Those are just a few of the words we use that cause us to ask for permission to do our jobs, which in turn gives the customer the right to say NO! And that, you don't want.

After you have written those down, have someone listen to you to hear if you're using any of those words and what the customer's response will be. Again, this will be a wakeup call for you, especially to hear how many time you're using words like that and the negative response you're getting from the customer.

It's All In The Words

Once you realize how often these words are used, it will help you to change them. Then you'll have to think of what to use in place of them. That will also be a challenge.

So, what can you say in place of those words? I'll give you some help. As I've said before. **You can't change their thinking until you change yours**. Thinking is what you're going to spend time working on. Trust me it will come. Here's one thing you can do that will help. Instead of saying MAY I? Say this.

Excuse me, would you mind terribly, if I asked you a question?

You'll need to say that to break their thinking. They will more often than not, say; **no, I don't mind.** What is important here is they got to say what they wanted to say; NO! The brain wanted to say no to a sales person and they did to you. The nice thing here is the no is positive and not negative. The defenses come down and the brain opens up for you to ask what you need too.

Now, you're in control of the sales. Now, say this. I was watching you and saw you pick up that bottle or shoe, or whatever the product was. Could you please, tell me what is it about that product that caused you to pick it up?

Now, they tell what it is that caused that process. They'll be selling themselves.That's what you want them to do anyway, sell themselves. All you have to do now is think of more

25

word changes you can make that will give you control of the situation.

People don't want to be sold and neither do you. People want to buy on their own and so do you. Let them think that they are and you'll have better sales.

What's important to remember is to break their thinking in order to control the sales environment. You need to have control.

"YOU CAN'T CHANGE THEIR THINKING UNTIL YOU CHANGE YOURS."

WHERE DID I LOSE THE SALE?

I often wondered when I was very active in selling at what point, did I lose the sale? Yeah! It occurred to me one day that the sale must have a sequence of event to go through before the close takes place.

That got me thinking about what salespeople go through in order to get the appointment, do the presentation and close the sale. I wanted to know what it was? What do we really go through in the sales process and does everyone go through the same thing?

What I decided to do was to list everything I could that transpired during the sales process and to see where in the process I could lose the sale.

Let's start the sale from the beginning and see where it goes. The first thing that happens is meet and greet the customer. Here is where you'll make the first impression with the customer. The first impression sets the stage of the sale.

Could you lose the sale at this step? I guess you could if the customer decides the first impression is not positive. SO, here is where you have to make sure you're as professional as you can be to insure the customer has a favorable impression of you in order to continue on.

Next would be the intro to you and the company you work with. This step would be important to let the customer know the company they'll be doing business with and the person conducting, representing the company. Could you lose the sale here? Yes, you can! The company has to provide the service the client needs and therefore the sales person has to make sure the needs are met as well and can be provided. The salesperson needs to make sure the right information is given and the right questions are asked to get the information from the customer in order to move forward.

The salesperson needs to develop the want need and desire from the customer in order to get the customer to move forward with the sale, the need for the product or service and to insure there are no objections that could stand in the way.

The responsibility here is yours. The responsibility will always be yours. You're the first line of the relationship you'll develop with the customer. It's up to you to insure the customer gets the best treatment possible. Remember, ask the right questions, get all the information you can that helps with moving the sale forward.

Keep the sale on track and let the customer know they're making all the right decisions for what they want and need.

What you say and how you say it will make all the difference in the sales process. It will always determine the direction of the sale.

Once you learn how, your sales will change for the better. Stay focused with what the objective is and listen to yourself as well as the customer and you'll always do fine. Remember;

if you don't like the response, change what you say or ask for the customer until you get what you need. This will take time because of your conditioning, but keep practicing and it will change.

YOU SOUND

Have you wondered or thought about how people sound when they talk to you? And whether their tone of voice has anything to do with the sales process?

Have you wondered how you sound to them? I remember one day while speaking with a customer trying to sell funeral arrangements, what the customer was hearing me saying. Then the wife said to me, you don't sound too sure of yourself.

When she said that to me it just struck a nerve. When I finished the appointment, I spent the rest of the day thinking about what she said. <u>YOU DON'T SOUND.</u> I thought how I must have sounded to all my customers and whether or not it made any difference in the sales process.

We get so caught up in the sales process we never think about what we say and how we say it to get the sale and especially how we sound trying to get it.

I know you can recognize what I'm saying because I'm sure you've been through the same thing. I'm sure in you speaking with people you heard the way they say things and you recognize how sincere they may be, or how excited they sound or even whether or not they were even interested in what you had to say. Tone of voice does play an important role in the sales process.

I'll give you three examples of how saying the same thing can sound. Put the emphasis on the words underlined when you speak them out loud and then ask yourself how does that sound to you? Remember, emphasis on the underlined word(s).

1. I can save you money.
2. I can - save you money
3. I can, SAVE YOU money
4. I CAN, SAVE YOU money.

Can you hear the difference in how you say the same thing? There is a difference in the tone in what you say and how you say it.

As you say things, there's a difference in the level of importance in your tone of voice, how you sound and what they hear.

I've noticed since shopping salespeople throughout the years there is very little difference in how salespeople speak to consumers. It seems no one or very few sales people have noticed the tone in which we speak and the effect it has on people.

Once I learned the importance it made in my sales presentation, my sales started to improve, coupled with everything else I learned my sales had to grow and they did.

I learned the importance in listening to people and how they sound, that gave me a better understanding in people, especially in what to look for in developing relationships in consumers.

That being said It; was just as important for me to be clear in what I said and to listen very carefully to what they said. Not only what I said but again, how I said it. Where and how was I putting the enforce in the communication.

It was very important in my tone of voice and how I wanted to customer to receive what I said.

Now that I discovered something else that affects my sales, I just wonder what else could there be that I might be missing? This was getting to be a very educational process for me.

I thought I was a pretty good salesperson. What I am realizing is that every little bit I can learn to help my sales grow, is worth the effort to learn.

Learning all these things has helped me tremendously as I'm sure it will help you. All you have to do is decide if you believe it and want to learn it.

HERE'S WHAT I HEAR

As we just talked about how you sound, I found myself learning another aspect of listening. While I was recording sales people during my training it was important for me to record them during the presentation training. This was a great learning experience for both of us.

When I heard things, I felt would give the customer reasons to say no I asked the sales person after a few seconds why they said it? Here's what I got back from them. I didn't say that! I said, wait a minute you did say that. Let me play this back for you. I did and sure enough they said it and then they argued with me they could swear they didn't say it.

I found that to be most interesting. I recorded more and more sales people bylistening to what they said and stopped them after I heard what they said again, that would give the customer a reason to say no.

Again, they would say no I didn't say that. When I played back the tape and they heard it, they said they really didn't remember saying that. This was very interesting to me to hear that from so any sales people denying what they said.

I came to the conclusion that sales people just weren't hearing themselves. They were either so conditioning in what they were saying, they didn't pay attention to themselves or they were so intent on getting to the sale they just didn't want to hear it and of course that is part of where the problem is.

I shopped and recording hundreds of salespeople and trained as many if not more and found this to be true in the majority of sales people.

Salespeople are in a rush to get to the sale they just don't know what they're missing out on.   If you don't fully understand what you're saying and how they're hearing it, you're losing sales you shouldn't lose.

Practice your listening skills on yourself, it will only make you better in sales and make sure they hear what you're really trying to say. Listen for what could give your prospect a reason to say no and change it.

GETTING BACK INTO THE SALE

We work very hard to earn a living y making sales, keeping customers happy, trying to get referrals and more sales. We do everything we can think of in how to increase income and our successes.

Sometimes to no avail. We 're not sure why or what happened but it just happens. We get into a sale and we know we're going to close it. We can feel it as we go along and then near the end when we say, all you need to do is just put your name here and we can get started, and then the customer says; let me think about it, or sleep on it, or talk to my spouse, partner.

I know this has happened to most of you if not all of you. When you reach that point in the sale all you can do is think about objections and how to overcome them. One thing you don't think about is how to get back in the sale. We don't even think about how too or why that would be so important, we're just focused on the sale and the objection(s) we're dealing with.

So that being said; can we do that? Can we get back into the sale before you loose it? And can we do it without dealing with the objection? Can we start over? Is it worth the trouble? It is and it's worth it.

Remember: Closing the sale is nothing more than finding out how soon they want to buy.

Neil Carlson

Sometimes, during the sales process, I knew I missed some information that was pertinent to the sales process. I just couldn't put my finger on it to move the sale forward and of course as usually happens, objections come up and now I'm lost. We know that most times objections are the cause of an unsold idea to buy and most times in my research we're the ones that cause that to happen and then we have to deal with it.

We have choices to make when we're in those situations. We need to stop and think about the whole process of the sale and at what point do we think about making changes in our presentations? It took a lot of thought and lost sales to think about an alternative way to work the sale. One question I asked myself was this. Do I have to deal with objections in order to move the sale forward? That question took quite a while to answer, but I did figure it out. I said don't answer the objection do something else, now what will you do?

And then I came up with it and it seemed to work. I kept trying it every time I ran into an objection that stopped the sales process.

Most often than not it worked for me. I really believe it can work for you as well.

Here's what I said. Once I was done when the customer either said NO, or gave me one of those objections I didn't want to deal with, I said; Fine or okay, Once I said that they knew I was done, and their defenses dropped down, at that point I would close my case and then say, Mr. or Mrs. Smith, would you mind terribly if I ask you a question before I

36

leave? They would always say, sure go-ahead. Could you please tell me what it was I did wrong? I just don't want to make the same mistake with the next customer I talk with?

Most every time they would say you did nothing wrong. Sometimes they would continue with, you did nothing wrong, we're just not ready to buy. As soon as they said that, I said, then what was it or is that I said that caused you to stop? Was it me or something I left out? Once they answered I was allow to continue or start over with more questions and or concerns. It gave me more info to start over and continue with the sale. It also gave me time to think about the sale, and which direction I could go, instead of just giving up.

All I wanted was another try at the sale. That gave me the opportunity to try again. The more try's you get the more opportunity to close the sale. If you don't have anything else to try, then try that. You just might find it will help you out.

Remember; When you've tried everything and you think you're done, there's nothing left, you're right, you are done.

What great about sales is choices. You'll always have choices to make in how you want the sale to go and when you make that choice, make it to help you move forward as much as possible.

Asking questions will bring you forward more than you can imagine. Just ask the right ones. I would put a list together based on your product or service and answer the questions the way you would want them answered,

CONFRONTING THE NEGATIVES

This is another area of the sales process we don't cover enough of. There seems to be a problem in this area that needs some work. One problem in this area is the sales person doesn't recognize the problem they have hear.

Part of this problem is salespeople don't recognize this as a problem and don't believe but they cause the problem.

Example of course is MAY I? Who causes the response from that? In sales, you usually do get what you ask for. We create the both positive and negative words in sales. We don't understand the consequence's this has on the sales process, otherwise we wouldn't have the problem. Furthermore, recognizing that it is a bigger problem.

We use words that greatly affect the disposition of the sales process because of the verbiage, we use. Here are a few examples of these and we'll talk about why they are problem words.

Here's the thing. We all use these even you. See if you can figure out why there so bad. Would You, Could You, Should You, How About, What If, Can I, Can you, What About, and of course MAY I, and IF I, IF You.

Why do you suppose these words have such a negative effect on the sales process?

Let me help you? What do these words imply, when used in the sales presentation?

WOULD YOU like too? HOW ABOUT, if I, and IF I DO THIS WILL YOU DO THAT? And so on.

These words are negative because it relinquishes control of the sale. You're giving the control to the customer and of course they're MORE than likely going to take it.

You set a negative tone and then create more problems when you do. And medoing this you create even more negatives like LET ME SLEEP ON IT. LET ME THINK ABOUT IT. I NEED A FEW DAYS. LET ME TALK IT OVER WITH MY, PARTNER/SPOUSE and so on. Any of these, ring a bell with you?

What about these? Would you like to get together on Monday or Tuesday?

Would you like to get together on Wednesday at 2:00 PM or would; Thursday at 10:00 AM be better for you? What you're doing here is giving a reason as well as a choice to move forward or stay still. You're also giving them a reason to put you off. Why do that?

I understand that giving a day and time frame may give you a better opportunity to get the appointment. What if the time frame is not comfortable for them? They're going to say no, they can't make it and then you're left with struggling for an appointment which is what you don't want to do. That being said what can you do?

Sometimes it's a tough thing to overcome because of circumstances.

My objective is to make the appointment setting process as comfortable as possible and easy for the customer to say yes to an appointment.

Here's what I've done to help with my appointments You need to determine that the customer wants the information to begin with and what the urgency is for the information. I would establish that first through a series of questions. Once I determined that, I would say something like this: Now that I understand you want and need to have the information to make sure you're making the right decision, what would be a comfortable day and time for us to go over it?

Most often than not I got the appointment. Sometimes I would say this as well: Mr. Smith, you've expressed a genuine interest in this information, is that correct?

They would say yes and I would then say; since that is the case I believe we need to make time to get together (go over the information) so you can make a logical decision on whether or not you even need it. Is that fair?

What's important here is what you're saying. First, you're taking the threat and fear of being sold away from the customer. The way you're doing that, is by saying, we need to get together. This also creates a since of urgency. Then, you're saying, so I can share this information with you. Sharing is letting the customer no there is no threat or fear of being sold.

Neil Carlson

You can make a logical decision (not a buying decision). A logical decision justifies the decision, and a rational decision without pressure.

A logical decision takes the pressure off the. It shows you're not trying to sell but trying to let them make the decision.

IS THAT FAIR?! This is the most important part of the question. You're asking them, if what you've said is fair? They'll justify it by saying yes, it's fair. And more often than not, you'll get your appointment.

Here it is again. **<u>We need to get together – so I can share this information with you – so you – can make a logical decision on whether or not you even need this. Is that fair?</u>** The threat and fear of being sold is gone.

It took me a long time to come up with this simple and effective way to break down barriers and take the threat and fear away from customers being sold.

In all my research, I have found that most people don't like being sold, and don't like sales people. Maybe you're one of those people as well. You like to buy on your own and don't like sales people either. Not that they're bad people but they're stereotyped as people that are pushy, lie, take advantage and so on. That's why we put sales people off.

If there's one thing I've remembered over the years and shopping consumers and salespeople alike, no one wants to be sold, not even you. I've made it a practice to let people buy on their own. You may want to think about that!

DOOR TO DOOR

This is a subject matter I find very few sales people are willing or even want to do.

As a matter of fact, you don't even find many sales trainers willing to talk about. At least I haven't found many

I don't know why that is, there's a lot of business out there to be had if you can just take the time to figure out how to do it.

A lot of salespeople tell me they would not do it. Most female sales people, if not all of them say, they don't know what's on the other side of the door and too dangerous to do it. That could be a very valid point and justifiable one.

There are few people that I know of that train in the art of door to door sales. Why is that?

When I was in the cemetery and funeral industry in order to get leads you had to go door to door to get leads. If you couldn't do that you went hungry. When I first started in the industry my manager said you'll need to go across the street and knock on door and tell that person they're going to pass away in 30 to 40 years and need to make arrangements now.

Well, I don't need to tell you I had a real problem with that. But in order to do the job I had to do it. It was a numbers game anyway and the more you did, sooner or later someone would listen to me. As you can imagine it would take a lot of doors for that to happen, so, I had to figure out a way to reduce the odds on the number of doors I would knock in order to set appointments.

What I did was to take all the information I could find in that field and I put it on the conference table and spread it out. After a while I found a book. I looked it over and asked the manager what it was used for?

He told me that when there is a death in the family, they give the book to the surviving spouse to fil out so the children wouldn't have to go through the same emotional experience she went through. AS soon as I heard that I went caching. I knew I had it. I went home and read did the book and inserted questions throughout the book and set it up as my presentation.

I then went out and took a book with me and knocked on the door. When the women answered the door, I told her I did a mailing in the neighborhood with this book and wanted to know if she got hers. Of course, I knew she didn't and she would say no. I didn't do the mailing either. I explained what the book was for and how it would save her hundreds if not thousands of dollars if there were an unexpected death in the family. I told her it was free and if she wanted one?

Most everyone said yes. I told her I would stop by later and bring one to her and did. I made the book my presentation, as I explained the pages in the book I knew if I could get to the last page all they had to do is ask me how much it cost at the end. Sure enough, most all of them did.

That's how I developed my door knocking skills to set appointments. I had to find something they wanted to have and develop questions I knew they couldn't answer and wanted the answers. I worked great for me and something like that can work for you.

I did all my door knocking during day light hours; so, I didn't have to worry about what was behind the door. Once I set the appointment it was easier from that point on.

As I've mentioned earlier, people don't want to be sold, they want to buy on their own. They need a reason to want what it is you have to offer and they want it to be simple to get it without all the baloney.

Remember, most all these people you'll speak with while you're in sales are just like you when it comes to salespeople. Don't be a sales person. Be a consultant, believe it and make them believe it, you'll do better only because your language will be better.

A PAT ON THE BACK

I've been in sales for over 40 years. I've spoken with thousands of people trying to learn what makes everyone tick. During that time frame, it's hard to remember how many times I got a pat on the back. Oh, I know I got some, just can't remember how many, can you. Can you remember the last one and the one before?

Why is it so hard to give a pat on the back? Sometimes the littlest things go along way and make people feel good. If you can't get one at work or not enough, then what can you do to give yourself one and feel good.

I gave myself a pat on the back by accomplishing goals or things of importance to me. My sense of success has always been on moving forward and achieving things that were hard for me. I've always believed there was a way around everything, everything within reason. You just have to put your mind to it and accomplish it. That I can say I have done. You can too if you believe you can.

When I accomplished something important to me, I rewarded myself with a gift of some kind. That was my pat on the back. We all need a pat on the back every now and then. Give yourself one you deserve it. Don't forget to give one to someone else.

OBJECTIONS - A NEVER ENDING BATTLE:

As we mentioned earlier and why people put you off because of what you say and how you say things, the same refers to objections and why they come up.

I firmly believe there's always a way to overcome objections or eliminate objections before they come up.

I also believe we are the ones that cause objections to happen. We create objection sin the customers mind from what we say and how we say things. As the customer processes the information we deliver to them, they determine the response from that information. Which in turn leads too objections or no objections.

A simple objection would no. Like you saying to a customer, may I help you? And, their response would be no. A simple objection that creates more problems than we want to deal with. But then again is that not something we asked for to begin with? We discussed this earlier and why saying what we say makes a big difference in the direction of the sale.

Here in objections we're talking about similar things that create different environments in the sales process. So, let's explore this more.

Objections are created by you. Not because you want them, because you don't think about them and how they come up. I've done tremendous research in this matter and find it to be true with everyone I have ever listened too or recorded from sales people.

I find that everyone in sales has the same problem. You all have to deal with objections in sales no matter what. So, what am I saying? What I'm asking is this. Do you have to have objections in the sales process? Or can you, drastically reduce the number of objections that come up during the sales process?

I believe there is. I believe we can eliminate objections before they come up and reduce the number of objections we get to make the sales process easier and more comfortable for both the sales person and the customer.

What does all this mean? Well, it means exactly what I've said. Objections in my opinion, are nothing more than a state of mind. A miscommunication in sales language between the customer and the sales person.

First, it starts with the beginning of the sale. What we're about to say and what we decide to say. I know some of you have done that. Thought about saying one thing and changed your mind and said something else. Why does this happen?

What caused you to change your thinking about what you were going to say and what you said?

Something happened in your brain that told you don't say what you were going to say, so you said something else instead and you did. Now the question is, did it work out, or didn't it? Was it a good thing or a bad thing? Did you make the right or wrong decision by changing what we're going to say? That's the part you didn't think about as to why you changed what you were going to say. A question here is, did you think about changing your mind and what caused it? Did you realize that you were thinking about changing your mind? Or did you just change it?

Like most people, and especially salespeople, we're so intent on what we want to do, we don't take the time to think about why we're doing it, or what's causing it to be done, we're just doing it. That may not make sense to you but I'm positive we don't question ourselves as to why we say what we say what kind of response we expect to get from it?

One day while in the sales process I said something to a customer and for some reason my brain said, why did you say that? I was taken back and then without a hitch, I thought about it and ignored the customer. It seemed like a long time but it was just a second or two. When I left the appointment got into my vehicle, and wrote that down.

When I got home, I sat down and started to think about it. I became obsessed with it. Why, was I not thinking about the verbiage I was using and the meaning of those words? The more I thought about it the harder it was to come up with an answer.

So, what was I going to do to make sure this didn't harm my sales? I decided to record as many conversations I had with sales people and consumers alike.

Then started to listen to them. One thing I discovered was that customers don't start the sales process with objections.

They don't say I want to think about it before you begin, or let me think about it before you start or even it cost too much before you tell me the price.

They just don't have any information to be able to do that, besides, it wouldn't make any sense for that to happen.

As we all know, objections don't come up until someone says something, we don't agree with, like or want to hear. Then we have to deal with objections. And that was the clue I needed to know.

Remember: You didn't have the objections going in, so why now?

Something has to be said for an objection to transpire. That's what I needed to listen for. What did I say that allowed the customer to change their thinking and hit me with an objection?

As I recorded and listened to my conversation that's what I had to find. And sure enough, I did hear it. I said this and they said that. It wasn't what I wanted to hear and furthermore it wasn't what I wanted the customer to say in response to what I said.

That is what really got me thinking about how to change my thinking about what I wanted to say and what kind of response I wanted to get. I kept track, I wrote things down I said that caused a negative response that offered an objection. I wanted to find something different to say that would give me the answers I wanted to hear. That took a lot of thought, especially to get back what I wanted the customer to say in response to what I said.

In time, I came up with enough things to say that would give me a more positive response I could work with.

Here's one thing I need that gave me an advantage over the customer to eliminate objections before they came up. Something you may want to try yourself to see how it works.

I would think about all the objections I would get like; I can't afford it! I need to think about it! I want to sleep on it! I need to talk to my spouse/partner first! I'm not sold on it! That one could be a tough one especially if you didn't do a good presentation and asked the right questions. Either way with those objections and there are more, I decided to make every objection into a question.

A question the customer needs to answer. From my research, I knew if they answered the question, they wouldn't come with it as an objection. Now think about that.

That's what I did. It took a while to come up with the right question or at least the question I was comfortable with the answers.

I'll give you an example; I want to think about it. A lot of people come up with that as an objection because it puts you off for more time before they need to make a decision. It ends the sales process as much as you'll try to over come that. Sometimes you can. Persistent can get you there and sometimes you can't.

What if in your conversation you asked a question pertaining to that objection ahead of time. Knowing that it might come up and heading it off before it does. Like saying; Most people I speak with about my product is to ask them, how long have you been thinking about this?

Their answer will give me some head way as to what to say next as it would you. They might just say, we've been thinking about this for a while now. Then I would say, why haven't you done anything sooner than now?

The reason I would ask that question was to hear were they're at in the buying process and to get rid of the thinking about it. Saying sooner than now implies they'll get it down I'm trying to change their thinking now.

They might even say; we've been thinking about it and just put it off until now or something like that, who knows. Either way it should get rid of, we want to think about it.

What you should do is think about all the objections you get and figure what kid of question you can come up with that they'll answer to get rid of the objection before it becomes an objection. You'll have nothing to lose and at least it will help you in the long run dealing with objections.

Sometimes objections come up because of what you leave out of the conversation as well as what we say in the conversation. Sometimes, simple words we use, we think are harmless. When in fact they're deadly.

That's why I recorded a lot of salespeople and myself. You need to know what you're saying.

Some people don't even hear what they say. I remember recording some salespeople and told them during their conversation they gave an out to the customer. Of course, they argued with me until I let them listen to the tape.

They swore they never said what they did, someone must have put that on the tape. They couldn't believe it.

If you can have someone record you, even if you're just practicing your presentation you'll still do it, say the same thing.

Remember; write it all down, the questions that is and answer them the way you want your customers to answer them. Go out and try it. If you don't get the answers you want then change the questions for the objections until you get the answers you want as I did in the example I showed you. It took me a while to get what I wanted. I had no examples to go by but I figured it out as you can and will if it's what you want to make sales a little easier for you and the customer.

Put your mind to it and you'll get what you need from your customers.

DON'T BE STEREO-TYPED

This has been one of the most inspiring journeys I've ever been on. Trying to found out why sales people create so many problems for themselves and just don't stop the see if it really is them causing the problem and why.

In all my research on the development of relationships between salespeople and consumers I've found that sales people will not take the responsibility of recognizing that they indeed do cause most of the problems they're going to encounter with consumers. I've never understood that. I've found that the majority of sales people never ask themselves about the problems they'll run into and what they can do about it to prevent those problems.

I'm willing to tell you that most, if not the masses of salespeople, have never taken the time to sit down before a presentation and asked yourself how do I want this presentation to turn out and what am I going to run into as far as problem areas such as objections, put-offs, excuses, presentation problems and so on.

Most sales people just move on and deal with the problems as they come up, which is fine, but wouldn't it seem more practical to head them off before they come up?

You all know what the problems are and you do know that eliminating the problems before having the problems is a much better way to do your selling.For some reason, we just don't do it. In-turn, we become stereotyped from with customers and unfortunately that is not a good thing. In my research, I asked consumers about you, you the sales person. I wanted to know how they felt about you and why?

I did a survey once at a shopping center outside a supermarket. I stood there with a pad of line paper and asked everyone I could that went in and came out, what was it they disliked and liked about sales people?

That was incredible the answers I got about you. I never felt so disappointed in sales people as I did that day. I stood outside and asked these questions. Tell me what it is that bothers you about sales people?

Here's what I got back.

1. They're dishonest.
2. They only want your money
3. The don't care about people.
4. They don't listen.
5. They don't pay attention.
6. They don't care about what you want.
7. They can't take NO for an answer (that could be good as well as bad).
8. They spend more time bothering people.
9. They always try to sell you something else.
10. They take too long.
11. They're usually pushy.
12. They always seem to be in a rush

Then I asked them this question: What is it you like about salespeople?

To say the least, it was very interesting to hear these answers. Not what I expected.

1. Sometimes they're nice.
2. Sometimes they're honest.
3. Some sales people are friendly.
4. Some sales people care, but most do not.
5. They'll try and sell you one thing as best than can.

Now, here's what's really interesting. I asked sales people how they felt about sales people as well. The surprise was they answered the same way as everyone else. Sales people didn't like sales people either. That was a big surprise.

I told salespeople about my research and how stereo-typed they were and how they felt about that? As surprised as I was, they weren't. They didn't seem bothered by it. I also asked them what they thought they should do about changing that?

They didn't seem to care much about that. It is what it is, they would say. I would ask them, when you go into a presentation do you ever think about how or what they think about you? Of course, they would say no, they never do. That is a true statement, they never do.

Thinking of that if it were my presentation, I would want to change the stereo-type about me. I would want people to think very highly of me and not so negatively. Thee sales people would even say; I'm not like that so I don't have to worry about it. I asked everyone that and for the most part they all said, I'm not like that, those are other sales people. But you fall into that category, you're stereo-typed like everyone else.

Isn't that sad to have to hear that about sales people? What a shame. Remember what I said earlier? People don't want to be sold they want to buy on their own.

Why don't we give them the chance to do that? I wrote years ago, People don't care about how much you know, only about how much you care.

That being the case you should remember this as well. You cannot change their thinking, until you change yours.

Get out of the stereotype. Be different than everyone else and let your customers know it. You'll be a lot better off I promise.

Remember: It's more important to know who they think you are.

TIME

What about time? Is time so important that we need to be conscious of it all the time?

What importance does time have in the sales process? Can time make or break a sale and if so or not, why?

When salespeople think about time, it's usually to set an appointment with someone to meet or to do a function based on time, time set.

When I was out shopping salespeople to see and hear what they were saying to set appointments with perspective clients there was always a common put off.

Here's what I hear from the clients:

"I'd love to get with you, I just don't have the time." "Unfortunately, my time is limited and just can't do it." I was wondering if now is the right time to do this?

Boy, time is one thing I just don't have right now, maybe later. I really can't give you any time right now. It's going to take too much time that I don't have and so on. We all get these from time to time.

A time problem or a sales people problem? My guess and I think you'll all agree is it's a sales problem.

I've analyzed this problem as a conditioning problem, as well as a sales problem.

Here's what I hear from salespeople; I promise I won't take up much of your time. If you could give me just a little bit of your time? I know you're very busy and don't have much time. What time is good for you? Is there a better time?

What about stated time? Let's get together on Tuesday at 3 or would Wednesday at 4 be better? Why do we do that? Why do we use time as an excuse; and they use time, as an objection?

Sometimes we try to use time as leverage. Sometimes we try to manipulate time to get what we want. One thing certain in my research is sales people seem to be causing more of the problem than customers do. Here's why I say this. Sales people have a tendency to give customers reason to be put off when it comes to time.

The way this happens is from the asking. That's right! It is the way sales people ask for appointments. Example: How about if we get together on Tuesday at 3 or would Wednesday at 4 be better?

Take a good look at that question and tell me what could be wrong with it. Read it over again and answer, what's wrong here?

Let me help you out. Where is the sense of urgency to even set the appointment? Where will this create importance to set the appointment?

Why is it important to create a sense of urgency to begin with? Think about how the question is being asked and go from there.

Remember; if it's not important to you, it's not important to them. When setting appointments, you have to make it important in order to create a sense of urgency.

The customer needs to know it's important to them and you as well to set the appointment. They want to make it a good experience to move forward, if they can't experience that or feel it, it won't happen, they won't set it.

More importantly, you're asking for permission to do your job. You should never do that, it gives the customer the right to say NO!

Do you remember we talked about that early on when we talked about MAY I? In the example you're doing the same thing, with different words. Using, HOW

ABOUT? You're doing the same thing.

When you're talking about time, we have this tendency to ask questions the same way and eliminate the importance of what we're trying to do?

Then you're giving choice, a choice of time that can also take away the sense of urgency. When you set time by the hour, people think it will be an hour long or more.

Some people just don't want to give that much time to salespeople. Not everyone will say no, but you don't want to lose sales because of it. Take advantage of everything you can to set appointments. Don't take it for granted that you can set appointments without understanding your customer.

Even when people agree to set doesn't mean they'll honor the time. I know we've all had that problem before. They set the appointment and don't show up and then give a reason why it's not important. And, that's the key word. IMPORTANT!

Why isn't it important to the customer any longer? We don't seem to ask ourselves why that is and what we can do to change it. We just keep going on the way we always do and things continue the way they always do.

Once you realize we need to change ourselves in order to change our customers we'll become better at what we do in all that we do. We'll take the customer at heart more.

So, what can we do about time to make it better for us to help our customers? One thing is to become more aware of the needs and concerns people have with sales people about their product or service. That alone will move you forward in the sales process. Setting a time is very important because of the time we're going to take from the customers day.

What happens when we set the appointment at 3:45 or 4:50? At this point, how long will the customer think the appointment is going to take? Will it be 15 minutes and ten minutes? Would someone be willing to give you that kind of time vs an hour. How much time would you give?

We have a tendency, to take more time than what we ask for. We all do it and that's what we train customers to understand. That's why it's hard to get the time. When we ask for a little amount of time it's easier for the customer to give that up. When you do this, just try and get ten minutes at a time. That way you'll get more of it. You've done this yourself. Asked for a little time and took a lot of time. You've given a little time and they took a lot of time.

The best advice I can give you for time would be the advantage you would have in using time to their advantage not yours. That way you might get all the time you need.

"YOU CAN'T CHANGE THEIR THINKING – UNTIL YOU CHANGE YOURS"

"NEVER EXPECT TO GET BACK – WHAT YOU'RE NOT WILING TO GIVE!"

HOW MANY TOPICS IN THE SALES PROCESS?

I wonder if anyone has ever taken the time to research this to find out? I bet not. I was curious about how many there are and if it's the same all the time in every sale.

This would be a great learning process for anyone in sale. It would be a great learning process to find out how the sale begins and where it ends with what process. Just thinking about it gets me excited just to figure out the process and to see what we can learn from this.

So, let's start at the beginning of the sale. Where is the beginning? Is it when we call the customer, email or visit to get an appointment? It really does not matter. What matters is what process we use to get what we want. That being the case what are the steps? What do we need to do to make it success?

I believe we need to follow some procedure, or do we? Let's see what wecan come up with. Here's what I believe we need to do. You may believe in something else and that's okay. Whatever works for you is fine, but sometimes there should be an alternative for what you do. I'm going to give you some throughout this book. Pick and choose your own. This is just a guide to try and help you along the way and make sales a more enjoyable process.

First Step: the beginning: The first exchange of information. Whether on the phone, email, letter or in person. I believe the objective here is to create an interest and a sense of urgency to take action.

Stimulate there thought process to want what you have to offer. This takes thought. How are you going to do that without giving them a reason to say no?

Second Step: What are you going to say to keep the thought process going in order to get the appointment?

Third Step: Once you've set the appointment and meet, how will you start your conversation that will get the client to continue listening to what you have to say to proceed ahead? Is what you say going to create interest and a sense of urgency to want more? How will you know?

Fourth Step: What's the next step? What direction do you need the sale to go and the customer to go? What is it that needs to be covered before you close and what is the process in doing so? How will you talk about your product or service? Will you be direct and just deliver the info or will you ask questions pertinent to what you have to offer? Will you prepare ahead of time?

Fifth Step: When you do your presentation, what do you expect the customer to feel as you go along? Will there be any high points to stimulate them and any questions to insure their attention? What kind of questions will you ask and why? Have you prepared for the answers you'll get and are they the answers you want?

Sixth Step: What's going to happen when you get your first objection? How will you overcome, or will you? Why will you have objections? Do you think you can have a sale without objections? How would you prepare for the objections you're going to get to ensure the sale will keep moving forward? How much time will you give to the process to make sure the customer doesn't have time to think about giving you objections?

Seventh Step: When is it time to close? Most trainers tell you to trial close. Is that a good thing or bad thing, you'll have to think about that? When was the last time you thought about how you wanted the sale and the close to go? Did you think it through or just do it.

Something I believe you should realize that sales is an action and reaction process with most sales people. I don't want to say everyone even though I believe it is everyone based on my research. How will you prepare to recognize this action and reaction while trying to close your sale and what will you do to insure it's a good close?

Eight Step: There is a danger in your process of closing the sale and that's the conditioning you have that sometimes hampers your ability to be great. I think it would be a good idea to look at yourself and see if you're doing some of the same things that are causing you lost sales.

Ninth Step: Preparing for Failure: What happens if I recognize I'm losing the sale? Where do I make my changes to continue on and with what do I do it?

We all lose sales, no one can sell everyone. All we can do is prepare for the unknow and the known. What do I mean?

Recognize what you say and do that causes lost sales for you and learn to change it.

Tenth Step: Close and Reclose: Why would it be important to close and reclose a sale? What does that mean and what would be the purpose of doing it?

Sometimes we need to insure we've done all we can do in the close and prevent buyer's remorse. We've all had it and have had to deal with it. How would you prevent buyer's remorse to keep from losing the sale?

These are some of the steps I have learned on my path in studying sales people. There all in the book and there all for you to learned what I have learned that's made me a better person and sales person.

I've spent my whole career in sales in trying to find out why things happened the way they did and if there is anything I could do to make it better.

I'm sharing this knowledge with you so you can learn about you. So, you can learn how things are and that things can be changed and you can change them.

As I've said, everything is in the book for you to take advantage of or not. You'll find out some very interesting things about yourself you probably never thought possible.

Think about what you do and who you are as a salesperson. You'll find that change will be the most difficult, but also the most rewarding.

WINNING THE OSCAR

Acting by definition; pretending to be something or someone you're not. I often thought about how and if acting plays a role in selling. My conclusion of course is yes, yes it does. The better the actor the more sales you can make.

But is that really the truth? Acting can be good and bad in sales.

Well, I guess it depends on how you look at the relationship of acting in sales. Does this mean you lie as much as you can to convenience people to buy?

No, I don't think so. It's not that at all. Then what is it? I believe acting is based on many areas of the sales process. Things like emotions. How do we use emotions when trying to sell a service or product? Is emotion something that plays a critical role in that process. I believe it does.

You create emotions for something that's moving you or the customer. As if you were selling a book of love poems. Definitely emotion there. How about someone's first automobile, where does emotion fit into that picture? I can hear you thinking about that now, and you're probably right.

Emotion can affect voice inflection. The tone of your voice and what you say to how you say it. Sometimes you can get people to tear up because of what you say and how you say it when selling a product or service.

If you've ever made final arrangements for expenses, for someone, there's a lot of emotion in that. Sometimes good and sometimes bad.

Sometimes we play on people's emotions, so they'll come to a decision on a product or service. For good or bad it does happen And, what about body language, that's a form of acting. How or what role does that play in sales.

You hear about body language all the time. Slumped over in a chair, arms crossed, head turned away, legs crossed and so on Body language let's us know if people are attentive or not, interested or not. There's a lot to read on body language.

And, of course eye contact. We've talked about eye contact. The more the better. People want to know you have their interest at heart and you're concerned about making sure they understand you as you're speaking by looking into their eyes when you do. What do you think they would think, if you were looking up at the sky while you were speaking to them?

They would probably think you have no real interest in the and didn't much care what you were saying or what they were hearing from you. Definitely, would not help your sale out very well.

Those are just three little things we mentioned. Emotion, Body Language and Eye contact. All part of your sales makeup and how you control them. When you have them all together would it be fair to say you're acting in a professional manner to cover the bases to get the sale? I think so!

Sometimes with just those three. you need to think about what you're doing and how you're doing to make sure everything is effective and fits where it supposed to fit.

And yet there is still more to the process. What about voice control, tone of voice and verbiage?

What role do those play in the sales process? Now those are a few I know you rarely think about all. I hear a lot of salespeople speak monotone throughout their presentation. Especially the pitch. It's the same throughout the saleSurprisingly enough, salespeople just don't pick up on it and it can make for a very boring presentation. One thing I truly recommend is that you record your presentation and LISTEN to it. If you don't like how it sound, they may not either. Time to put some voice inflection in it.

Sound can and does make a presentation good or great. And verbiage does the same thing. What you say and how you say can make all the difference in the world in the sales process. You do want to be great at what you sell!

I'll tell you one thing I did to improve my overall sales skills and it truly helped me out. I TOOK AN ACTING CLASS, to deal with emotion, voice inflection and body language.

Everything plays an important part of the sales process, everything. If one aspect of the process is off or missing, losing the sale becomes greater.

I'm assuming YOU want every aspect of the sales process to be as good as you can make it. After all, it's your money.

You might want to consider learning more about how everything plays a role what your product requires to insure better sales.

And what about verbiage? How do words play a role in what you sell? This one I strongly believe you need to improve on, strongly. You might be asking yourself, what am I talking about and that's ok?

Let me see if I can give you examples of what I mean. You might say to a customer; that sounds good and I continued with the sales process. Not good, not bad, it is what it is. Where I would say; "Hears what I hear you say". And repeat what they said. Why would I do that? YOU, answer the question.

Or, the customer might say; I'm looking for a computer. And you might say; That's great, let me show you what I have. Where, I might say; Well, we can solve that problem, would you mind if I asked you a question before we begin? Why would I do that? YOU answer that.

Verbiage plays an important role in the process. It can either give you control or take it away from you. It can move you forward in the sale or hold you stagnant in the sale.

I guess it really depends on where you want to go with the sales and how you want to go to insure you get the sale.

I'm not saying if you don't do these you won't get the sale. You will get sales you're getting sales now and probable not doing all those steps. What I'm saying is how hard do you want to make the sales process and how many sales do you want to have?

Me, I wanted all the sales and all I could get. Sales was hard enough and I didn't want to make it any harder than it was. I wanted this to be easy, as easy as I could make it. 'IT'S ALL IN THE WORDS'.

ONLY YOU CAN DO IT

There's, thousands of us out there trying to find the "Golden Bullet or Phrase" that will WIN our customers over in buying our product or service.

Unfortunately, it seems to be incredibly hard to find, if it exists at all. In all the research, researching you, I have never found nor have I ever heard of it. But there is one thing for sure, it seems to be more than one thing, one phrase or sentence.

The magic seems to be in what you say and how you say it as we have discussed.

I have come, to the conclusion it truly is in the words you use, that really makes all the difference in the sales process. It becomes a combination of words phrases and sentences all rolled into what you're going to say during your conversation with the client that will make or break the sale.

If you leave a phrase or sentence out and even a word or two, you'll lose the sale or get objections you didn't expect to get. Something happens that throws every off and it leaves you wondering; What Happened? I had it, I knew it, I was right there with it, and it's gone.

Only you can make it and only you can make it. Don't blame the customer they're just following your language, after all, that's what there used too and what they have been trained to do. You remember when I said you wear two hats and you're just selling with the wrong one on? Well, that will always be the case.

The difference you make in them, will be because of the difference you make in yourself. As in the title; You need to change your thinking in order to change there's.

Think about that.

WHY THIS BOOK

I was born in Massachusetts way back when. Never had a thought of what I would do when I grew up. I only started that thought process when I got out of the service. Little did I know then I would end up in sales.

I've been in sales now for over 52 years. I believe; I've strived to be as good as I could be and learned something in that amount of time.I will say this; I've learned more about people than anything else in my career. I've always made it a point to find better ways to sell and work with Customers. To find what it is that makes them tick. Why do they think the way they do and what causes them to respond in so many ways?

What is it that brings out the negatives in their sales language and cause, negative responses it causes? That prompted all my research in finding out what it is that salespeople say and do that cause customers to respond the way they do.

I've shopped over 6000 salespeople all over the country and recorded too many to remember. My purpose was to find a common denominator in sales people. My discovery was that salespeople were giving customers reason to put off the sales process and end the sale. A wakeup call.

And even more important, sales people never sopped to try and figure why this happened as you will read about.

I guess the most important lesson I've learned is our conditioning and how it hampers every aspect of the sale.

I only ask that you keep an open mind and try to put yourself in the customers Shoes, and how similar your thinking is with theirs. If you do, you'll learn a lot about you and your sales will improve.

Good Luck and Good Selling. It will always be in the words you use.

Printed in the United States
By Bookmasters